Avoid being a
Victorian Servant!

WANTED

In a gentleman's family, a short distance from London, a good parlour maid. She must be accustomed to the care of plate, glass, and waiting at table. There are four sitting rooms to keep clean, with fires. A thoroughly respectable, steady young woman, of religious character, desired.

The Danger Zone

Written by
Fiona Macdonald

Illustrated by
David Antram

Created and designed by
David Salariya

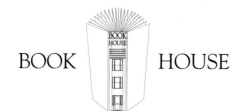

BOOK HOUSE

Contents

Your daily duties...
You will get up at 5.30 am and clean the kitchen floor. At 6.00 heat water for washing. Wake the senior servants at 6.30, and get the fires lit. Lay servants' breakfast and deliver breakfast to the nursery. At 7.30 prepare hot water and tea trays for the family and empty the chamber-pots. At 7.45 have your own breakfast. Say your prayers at 8.30 (remember to pray for your employer's health and prosperity). At 9.00, serve the family breakfast and clear the table at 9.30. At midday, have your lunch, help with the servants' lunch and serve the nursery meal on a tray. At one o'clock, serve the family lunch and clear the lunch table at 2.30 pm, then you can have a rest and do some mending. The family take afternoon tea at 4.30, so prepare the tea trays. Servants' tea is at 5.30, but you will also have to serve the nursery tea. At 6.00 lay the table for the family dinner and help prepare food in the kitchen. Dinner is served at 7.00 sharp. Serve dinner and clear up before having your own supper at 9.00. You can go to bed at 11.00. Your pay will be twenty pounds a year, board included...our housemaids are always called Mary. You will answer to this name when called.

A few rules:
1. When you're spoken to, keep your hands still and always look at the person addressing you.
2. Never let your voice be heard by the ladies and gentlemen of the household, unless they have asked you a question. Even then, always speak as little as possible.
3. In the presence of your mistress, never speak to another servant, or to a child, unless absolutely necessary.
4. Never talk to a lady or gentleman, unless to deliver a message or to ask a necessary question.
5. Items that have been dropped, such as spectacles or handkerchiefs, should be returned to their owners on a tray.
6. Always respond to an order or reprove, and always use the proper address: 'Sir', 'Ma'am', 'Miss' or 'Mrs', as the case may be.
7. Never offer your opinion to your employer.
8. If you meet one of your betters in the house or on the stairs, you are to make yourself as invisible as possible. Turn yourself towards the wall and look away.
9. Never say "good morning" or "good night" to your employer, except in reply to a greeting.
10. If you are required to walk with a lady or gentleman, always keep a few paces behind.
11. You are expected to be on time for meals.
12. You can have no visitor into the house or the Servant's Hall, without the consent of the Butler or Housekeeper.
13. Followers are strictly forbidden. If you are found meeting with followers, you will be immediately dismissed.
14. Breakages or damages in the house will be taken from your wages.
15. You can go to church on a Sunday, but only if your chores are done – and no dallying on the way back!

And don't forget...
If the bell rings once, you are wanted. The mistress does not like to see servants. Starch your underskirt so it rustles when you're coming and the mistress can look away! You must not go into the family areas of the house without permission – inside or outside – except on business. If you are seen by a member of the family, you will stand still and look at the floor – or turn to the wall. Oh yes, and stay away from the windows so you are not seen!

Author:

Fiona Macdonald studied history at Cambridge University and at the University of East Anglia. She has taught in schools, adult education and universities and is the author of numerous books for children on historical topics.

Artist:

David Antram was born in Brighton, England, in 1958. He studied at Eastbourne College of Art and then worked in advertising for fifteen years before becoming a full-time artist. He has illustrated many children's non-fiction books.

Series creator:

David Salariya was born in Dundee, Scotland. He has illustrated a wide range of books and has created and designed many new series for publishers both in the UK and overseas. In 1989, he established The Salariya Book Company. He lives in Brighton with his wife, illustrator Shirley Willis, and their son Jonathan.

Editor:

Michael Ford

Consultant:

David Fraser,
Judge's Lodgings, Powys

I am the housekeeper. I am always right!

Published in Great Britain in 2005 by
Book House, an imprint of
The Salariya Book Company Ltd
25 Marlborough Place, Brighton BN1 1UB

S A L A R I Y A

HB ISBN-13: 978-1-904642-75-6
PB ISBN-13: 978-1-904642-76-3

Please visit the Salariya Book Company at:
www.salariya.com

Visit our website at **www.book-house.co.uk**
for free electronic versions of:
You wouldn't want to be an Egyptian Mummy!
You wouldn't want to be a Roman Gladiator!
Avoid joining Shackleton's Polar Expedition!
Avoid sailing on a 19th-century Whaling Ship!

A catalogue record for this book is available from the British Library.

Printed and bound in China.
Printed on paper from sustainable forests.

Reprinted in 2011.

Dedicated to the memory of
Beatrice Corbet Salariya
1907-2004

Introduction

You're a bright young girl, aged 12 years old. You live in Britain, around 1885. For the past 120 years, new industries have transformed the nation. Now it is busy and confident, with shops, factories and big cities. Railways and steamships link British ports with a vast empire overseas. Queen Victoria – one of Britain's greatest rulers – is on the throne.

Ding!

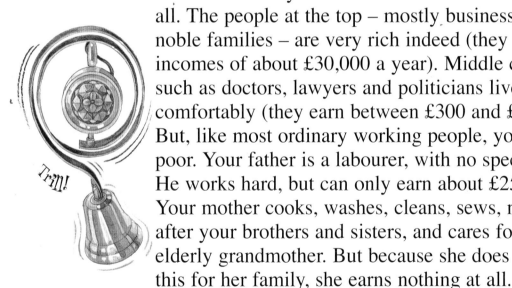

Trill!

Britain is very rich. But this wealth is not shared by all. The people at the top – mostly businessmen and old noble families – are very rich indeed (they have incomes of about £30,000 a year). Middle class people such as doctors, lawyers and politicians live very comfortably (they earn between £300 and £800 a year). But, like most ordinary working people, your family is poor. Your father is a labourer, with no special skills. He works hard, but can only earn about £25 a year. Your mother cooks, washes, cleans, sews, mends, looks after your brothers and sisters, and cares for your elderly grandmother. But because she does this for her family, she earns nothing at all.

Life could be worse. You have a small, cramped home, plain, simple food to eat, and old, patched clothes to wear. Money is always scarce and there is none saved for emergencies. You're growing up fast, and want to help. It's time you got a job!

Ting-a-ling!

From country to city

Alternative careers:

Before deciding to be a servant, consider other careers. shop work is exhausting (all day on your feet); farm work is dirty; factory work is dangerous.

Shop assistant

Grunt

Oink

Farm hand

Argghhh!

Factory worker

Y ou're bright, keen and lively, but you haven't had much education. Your parents could not afford to send you to school. But you've learned to read and write at classes run by a charity. You know how to care for children, you can count and you can sew. So what kind of job might you do?

Sadly, for most young girls, there is not much choice. Your family wants you to be a servant (13% of the female population in Britain are in domestic service). Without servants, rich people could not lead such comfortable lives. But the pay is bad, the hours are long, and there is not much personal freedom. Is it really the right job for you?

At least it's only once a month!

Handy hint

Go to Sunday School! It will teach you how to read and write, as well as learning about religion.

Employers set very high standards when selecting servants. So don't be surprised if they inspect you closely and ask lots of questions. They'll want you to be neat and pretty, to look pleasant around their home. They'll expect you to be strong, with the stamina to survive. They'll check that you're clean and healthy – they don't want you spreading disease. And they'll insist that you're obedient and show the right attitude. No-one wants a servant who is cheeky or rude! Remember – always call them 'Sir' or 'Madam', and never speak until you are spoken to.

Let's see your teeth, little one!

TWEENIES. You may not be a maid straight away, you might have to work as a tweeny for a while. A tweeny is a kind of servant's servant who helps behind the scenes. You can expect to earn only £4-£8 a year!

Dressed for the job:

Lace-trimmed cap – the sign that you are a servant

Long hair tied neatly back (No fringe – or you'll be sacked)

Stiff, starched collar

Close-fitting buttoned bodice

Tight waist (achieved by wearing a whalebone corset) – most uncomfortable

Apron – protects your clothes

Long skirt – heavy and bulky, it gets in the way when you work

Black woollen stockings – they itch, and often need mending

Boots – heavy, well polished and hard-wearing (Fashionable footwear is not allowed)

Handy hint

Don't be surprised if your employer calls you by a new name. They may not like the one your parents gave you.

From top to toe:

SOME EMPLOYERS supply uniform, but others expect you to provide your own suitable clothes. It could take two years of hard saving to be able to afford these clothes! Either way, you'll have to make and mend your own underwear – chemise (vest), drawers (long knickers) and layers of petticoats. But remember, jewellery and make-up are strictly forbidden.

BE OBEDIENT! If not, you'll be punished. You might not get any food or pay. Or you might lose your job. And if you break anything, it will be deducted from your wages.

Will you find a good situation?

Are you a hard worker, and fond of company? Then you might like to work in a huge stately home – with about 50 other employees! At first, the staff may ignore you, while they get on with their own work. But you'll soon make friends with other young servants – and you'll never, ever, be lonely.

Maybe you're shy and nervous, and would prefer a quieter life. There are jobs for solitary servants, running small family homes. But be warned! Single-handed servants are often cruelly overworked.

How to find a job:

IT'S NOT ALWAYS EASY to find a job. Have you visited one of the new staff agencies? They send servants to work all over the country – and sometimes overseas. Sometimes these agencies are run by charities, such as the 'Metropolitan Association for Befriending Young Servants', who, by the mid-1880s, operated 25 branch offices and claimed to place 5,000 girls in service per year.

TRY a mop fair in a country town. Employers go there to inspect new workers.

READ advertisements in the newspapers. Employers list their needs in print.

Handy hint

Get references from anyone you've already worked for. You'll find it hard to get a job without them.

WANT TO LEARN SPECIAL SKILLS, such as cooking for parties? Watch the senior servants in a grand stately home (above) to see how jobs are done.

HAPPIER JUST DOING everyday housework? A smaller home (right) is the place for you!

LOOK OUT for cards in shop windows. You'll find all kinds of jobs advertised there.

ASK domestic staff at local houses if there are any vacancies for young maids.

RELY on charity. Do-gooders like to help poor girls find 'respectable' work.

Can you get up early ...and stay up late?

Your employers will expect you to work long hours – just to make life easier for them. You'll have to get up at dawn to light fires and boil water for washing. Then you'll have to help cook and serve their breakfast, before eating your own. At night, you'll have to sit and wait until your employers have gone to bed. You might be needed to answer the door, or to carry out any orders. Your own bedroom is cold and damp, and your bed is hard and lumpy. But you'll be so exhausted by the time you get there that you'll soon sleep, anyway!

Busy all day long!

Morning:

Cleaning the stairs

Pumping water

Boiling kettles

Opening shutters

5 am 11pm... or later

Handy hint

Be careful with candles or you'll burn the house down.

It's hardly worth getting undressed!

Evening:

Tidying the kitchen

Washing the scullery floor

Setting mousetraps

Phew!

Locking doors

Are you familiar with lamps and fires?

IT TAKES STRONG MUSCLES and a delicate touch to heat and light a Victorian family home. Be sensible, and you should stay safe. But accidents will happen.

Oil lamps are very fragile.

Axes are sharp – watch your aim!

Whack!

t's your task to heat and light your employer's home. Can you trim the wicks (burning bits) on oil lamps, and replace the mantles (glowing bits) on gas ones? Gas lighting was introduced into servants' halls in the 1860s to test that it was safe enough for their masters! Remember, though: gas and oil lamps are thought to taint food, so use beeswax candles to light the dining room. Can you clean ash and cinders from yesterday's fires, and re-light them, and keep them burning? Can you carry enough coal to stoke the huge iron range (stove), so that it stays hot enough to cook on? Stoves need a great deal of care and attention. Cast-iron rusts very easily and needs to be cleaned regularly with emery paper and polished with a leather pad, before being given a coat of black lead.

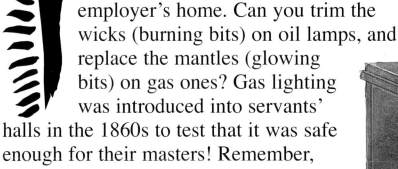

Coal is heavy, dirty and dusty.

Oil lamps smoke!

Coal cellars are dark, cold and smelly.

Are you squeamish about slops?

Bothered by bugs!

Bedrooms should be peaceful places to sleep and dream. But bugs make them a nightmare! Insects breed in the soft, cosy furnishings.

Fleas suck blood

Bed bugs bite badly

Lice make you itch like mad

Your employers will not mention this job, but you know you will have to do it. Every morning without fail you must remove 'used' chamber-pots from each bedroom without being seen and empty the contents down the nearest drain! If your master wants a bath, you have to heave hot water up the stairs in heavy cans to fill it. Afterwards, you carry the cold, dirty water back down stairs to empty into the drains. Servants aren't so fortunate – you'll be expected to have a bath in the kitchen. If you are lucky though, you will have a 'housemaid's cupboard' on each landing. These are special cupboards with taps and drains down which you can pour dirty water and the contents of a chamber-pot.

BUGS live in beds and under wallpaper.

Aaahtchooo!

FEATHER BEDS and quilts need to be aired daily.

THERE MAYBE a lavatory in the house. But why should your employers walk through a cold house at night when they have you to empty their chamber-pots!

Iffy whiffy

Niffy pong

Noxious niff

Handy hint

Use a red-hot poker to sizzle bugs in cracks in walls.

Bump!

WATCH OUT for rugs – or you'll trip.

DON'T POLISH the floor under rugs or they'll slip.

MIRRORS can be cleaned with vinegar and water.

Are you strong enough to sweep and clean?

Rich Victorians like their homes to be clean and to look tidy. But they don't expect to do any housework themselves. It will be your job to wash muddy floors, sweep dusty stairs, clean huge glass windows, shake and beat the carpets, polish heavy wooden furniture, wipe down walls and paintwork – and scrub the stone steps and pavement outside the front door. The work is exhausting – and you'll have to do it by hand. Your only tools will be brushes, mops, dusters, carpet-beaters and buckets of soapy water. When you've finished it, you'll also have to tidy books and papers, hang up clothes, and pick up children's toys.

A week of cleaning:

YOU'LL HAVE TO clean the kitchen and scullery every day. But employers expect you to keep all the other rooms spotless, too. Draw up a rota, so you don't forget!

Handy Hint 2

To brush dust from the carpets, scatter damp tea leaves and then brush them up.

Monday – Parlour

Tuesday – Dining room

Whoosh!

Wednesday – Nursery

Thursday – Front door and stairs

Friday – Spare bedroom

Saturday – Study

Do you know how to cook?

Do you know how to skin rabbits and pluck chickens? Could you make your own ice-cream, or bake bread? Can you bear to peel tonnes of potatoes, or stand for hours stirring soups and stews? Yes? Then consider a cooking career! You'll first need to work as a scullery maid, washing greasy dishes and pans all day. But with luck, you'll move on to be kitchen maid, helping the cook. After many years, you'll learn enough to be a cook yourself, with servants of your own. Cooks are in charge of ordering the exact amount of provisions to feed the household.

I can sell any leftover fat to the cookshop.

Cooks also have to:

Maybe cold consomme to start?

PLAN MEALS with employers, for family, guests and servants.

ORDER FOOD and get it delivered from markets, shops and farms.

This fish is not fresh

SUPERVISE kitchen maids to make sure the washing up is done after every meal.

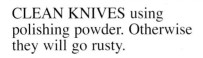

CLEAN KNIVES using polishing powder. Otherwise they will go rusty.

COOKS might have to polish tableware, but this is usually a butler's job.

KEEP A DOG and a cat. Without them, rats and mice will creep into the kitchen, eat stored food and spread disease.

Waiting on hand and foot

Where's my tea-tray It's almost five o'clock!

Trill!

Perhaps you'd like to be a parlour maid? That's a superior kind of servant, trusted to serve meals and greet visitors. Compared with the other servants' work, you may think the job sounds pleasant. There's no dirty

SAFE PAIR OF HANDS? Carry food to dining room, and serve it while it's hot.

NEAT AND NIMBLE? Lay the table before each meal, and clear away afterwards.

Ding! Ting-a-ling!

Handy hint

Walk, don't run, when answering bells, or you'll trip over your long skirt.

work involved, and you wear a stylish lace-trimmed uniform. But, even so, the work is not easy! You could never relax – you're always on call. You'd need great self-control to stay polite and calm, however badly you are treated. And you'll spend all day from dawn to dusk without the chance to sit down!

Always be polite when answering the door to guests.

FETCH AND CARRY. Deliver mail and newspapers to your employer, on a silver salver.

23

Are you handy with a needle?

If you don't like sewing, be grateful you don't work as a seamstress. They sit for hours on end in the same position and suffer terrible ill-health and eye-problems.

Like other girls in Victorian Britain, you make and mend your own clothes. But rich women and their daughters have specialist servants to help them. These 'ladies' maids' stitch, clean and care for their employers' beautiful frocks, style their hair, polish their shoes, tidy their bedrooms – and even help them get dressed! If you have good taste, an eye for fashion, and excellent sewing skills, this might be the job for you! Not keen on fashion? Not thrilled by frills? Then say you can do 'good plain sewing'. Remember, all the sheets, towels, quilts, curtains and tablecloths used in rich households are made by hand!

Handy hint

Tell your employer about sewing machines. They're the latest technology and will save you hours of work.

Put that down – don't get ideas above your station!

Prospects for promotion

RISE THROUGH THE RANKS of servants, from humble washerwoman to respected housekeeper. Each servant's work is important, but some have more pleasant – and better paid – tasks than others. Below you can see a guide to rough yearly salaries c. 1880.

If you decide to become a servant, what will your future hold? Will you spend all your life in a tiring, boring job? Or will you make progress, and be promoted? With hard work and good luck, you might win better pay, higher status, and more job satisfaction. You may even end up as a housekeeper – the best servant job of all. Then, you'd be in charge of all the other servants, and you'd control the household budget, too. Employers would rely on your skills, and everyone would respect you. You will have your own sitting room, and best of all you won't have to wear a uniform.

Washerwoman, £5

Scullery maid, £8-£12

Housemaid, £20

Parlour maid, £10-£20

Nursery maid, £20

Ladies' maid, £50-£60

Cook, £50

Housekeeper, £40-£60

Or get married to escape?

Most employers forbid 'followers', as boyfriends are called. But, like other female servants, you'll find ways to make friends with young men. You'll get to know gardeners, stable lads, delivery boys and footmen who call at the house where you work. You'll meet brothers of other servants, or smile at handsome strangers as you walk to church on Sundays. Many girls can't wait to get married and leave work. They hope marriage will bring them love and the freedom to run their own lives. But be warned! You might find that married life is just as hard work as being a servant.

Can't stand being a servant any longer?

GO HOME to your family. But will they be pleased? They might not have food to feed you, or room for you to stay.

BEG ON THE STREETS. But this is shameful, dangerous, and against the law. You'll also get horribly cold and wet.

DO ODD JOBS, like knitting or mending. These use your skills, but rely on good eyesight and are badly paid.

FOLLOWERS ARE STRICTLY FORBIDDEN! Your employers will dismiss you if they find you with a boyfriend. They think followers are immoral, and more importantly interrupt your work. So take care! Be discreet! And remember – if you get pregnant, you will certainly lose your job.

Handy hint

Work hard and be faithful to your employer. They may give you a small pension to help you survive when you're too old to work.

Waaaghhhh!

GO TO THE WORKHOUSE – a place for poor people, run by local government. But life there is grim and miserable.

Glossary

Black lead Polish used on iron grates and ranges. It contains lead (a metal) and gives a shiny black finish.

Bodice The upper part of a woman's dress.

Chamber-pots Large china containers, used as lavatories.

Chemise A sleeveless top or vest.

Cinders Partly-burnt coal, found at the bottom of fires.

Do-gooders People who try to help others in a bossy or interfering way.

Drawers Long knickers.

Emery paper A stiff paper coated with powdered emery (a type of mineral) or sand, and used for polishing grates and stoves.

Empire Foreign lands ruled by a powerful country.

Followers Boyfriends.

Footman A male servant. He served food, ran errands, and answered the door.

Governess A woman teacher who gives lessons to children of rich families in their own homes.

Grates Metal baskets, used to hold burning coal in fireplaces.

Mantles Small ball-shaped nets made of special chemicals. When heated in a gas lamp, they glow very brightly.

Mop fair An open-air gathering, attended by servants looking for work, and employers hoping to find servants.

Nursery Rooms for babies and young children in a large house. Used for sleeping, eating, studying, and playing.

Parlour Living room.

Pension Money paid to a worker who has retired.

Range Very big stove, used for cooking and heating water.

References Reports on workers by their former employers.

Scullery Room next to a kitchen, used for washing dishes, cleaning dirty foods (such as vegetables), and sometimes for washing clothes.

Slops Dirty water. Also, the contents of used chamber-pots.

Staff agencies Offices which put employers looking for servants and servants seeking work in touch with one another.

Stamina Strength and staying-power.

Starched Stiff and crisp.

Stately home A very large, grand house, often belonging to a noble family.

Sunday school Classes on Sundays, run by Christian organisations to help poor children learn to read and write.

Tweeny A servant of very low standing who worked behind the scenes, serving the other household servants.

Wicks Strips of woven cloth (about 4 cm wide). When soaked in oil and burned in lamps, they gave a warm, soft light.

Workhouse A huge, grim work place, where very poor people could get food and shelter. In return, they had to work long hours doing hard, boring jobs.

Index